MARVELS and MYSTERIES

MUMMIES

Paul Mason

Smart Apple Media

This edition first published in 2005 in the United States of America by Smart Apple Media.

Smart Apple Media
1980 Lookout Drive
North Mankato
Minnesota 56003

First published in 2005 by
MACMILLAN EDUCATION AUSTRALIA PTY LTY
627 Chapel Street, South Yarra, Australia 3141

Visit our website at www.macmillan.com.au

Associated companies and representatives throughout the world.

Library of Congress Cataloging-in-Publication Data

Mason, Paul, 1967-

Mummies / by Paul Mason.
    p. cm. – (Marvels and mysteries)
    Includes index.

    ISBN 1-58340-786-3

    1. Mummies—Juvenile literature. I. Title.
    GN293.M372 2005
    93'3—dc22

                                                        2005042862

Edited by Vanessa Lanaway
Text and cover design by Karen Young
Page layout by Karen Young
Illustrations by Jacqui Grantford
Maps by Karen Young
Photo research by Jes Senbergs

Printed in China

Acknowledgments
The author and the publisher are grateful to the following for permission to reproduce copyright material:

Front cover photograph: Mummies at Asaro caves, Papua New Guinea, courtesy of Corbis.

Texture used in cover and pages, courtesy of Photodisc.

Ancient Art & Architecture, pp. 26, 27; The Art Archive, pp. 12, 25; Corbis/APL, pp. 4, 6, 7, 10, 11, 13, 14, 16, 20, 21, 22, 23, 24, 28, 29; Kobal, p. 5; Naturfoto-Online/Mikhailov, p. 18; Science Photo Library, pp. 15, 17, 19.

CONTENTS

GLOSSARY WORDS

When a word is printed in **bold**, you can look up its meaning in the glossary words box, and on page 31.

TIME

Some of the stories in this book talk about things that happened a long time ago, even more than 2,000 years ago. To understand this, people measure time in years Before the Common Era (BCE) and during the Common Era (CE). It looks like this on a timeline:

2000 1500 1000 500 0 500 1000 1500 2000 2500

Years BCE   **Years CE**

Mysterious MUMMIES

People have always been fascinated by mummies, which are **preserved** bodies. Mummies can turn up in the most unexpected places, from melting **glaciers** to **peat** bogs. Some mummies have lain for hundreds of years in their tombs, surrounded by fabulous treasures, before being discovered.

Some mummies are very old—they can be up to 7,000 years old. Until recently, no one knew who made the mummies, or how. This knowledge had died out with the people who created them. Piecing together clues from the past has helped us to discover the mysterious secrets of the mummies.

⋯➤ Our fascination with mummies began just over 200 years ago. French soldiers who invaded Egypt brought back stories of mummified bodies. Sometimes they even brought back the mummies themselves!

FACT FILE

The Oldest Mummies

- Chinchorros mummies from Chile—up to 7,000 years old.

- Ancient Egyptian mummies—up to 6,000 years old.

- Ötzi the Iceman—about 5,300 years old.

A scene from *The Mummy Returns*. Filmmakers have always found mummies inspiring. Could these mysteriously preserved bodies somehow be brought back to life, to wage war on the living?

Tomb robbers!

The mummified pharaohs of Ancient Egypt were buried alongside amazing treasures. Tomb robbers would try to break in and steal the treasure, though this was punishable by death. The pharaohs were thought of as gods. They often placed a curse on tomb robbers. One warning carved on a tomb threatened robbers: "He shall not reach his home. He shall not embrace his children. He shall not see success."

Wealthy mummies

Some ancient groups of people mummified their dead leaders. Often these mummies were surrounded by things of great value. The Ancient Egyptians buried their **pharaohs** with all sorts of treasure. The mummified leaders of the Inca people in South America were kept in a great palace, surrounded by luxury.

GLOSSARY WORDS

preserved	kept from changing
glaciers	giant build-ups of compacted snow and ice in valleys
peat	a thick, dark-brown soil that can be burned on a fire
pharaohs	rulers of ancient Egypt

What makes A MUMMY?

How mummification happens

Some mummies are created on purpose, by living people. Other mummies are made accidentally, by nature. The main causes of mummification are:

- extreme cold
- heat or dryness
- chemical reaction, for example, when the chemicals in a peat bog cause mummification.

A mummy is a preserved body. Usually when living things die they start to rot, until all that is left is the skeleton. When a body is mummified this does not happen. Mummification can be deliberate or natural. Natural mummification usually happens when a body is frozen or preserved in a peat bog and does not decompose.

Deliberately made mummies

For thousands of years, some groups of people have deliberately mummified their dead leaders or relatives. From Ancient Egypt to Chile and China, dead leaders were mummified and honored. In Australasia, Europe and North America, people's relatives were mummified so that their presence could remain on Earth.

....➤ These resting figures are the mummies of people killed in battle and village leaders. They sit on scaffolding at the Asaro caves in Papua New Guinea. The mummies were dried by the air and are about 300 years old.

Natural mummies

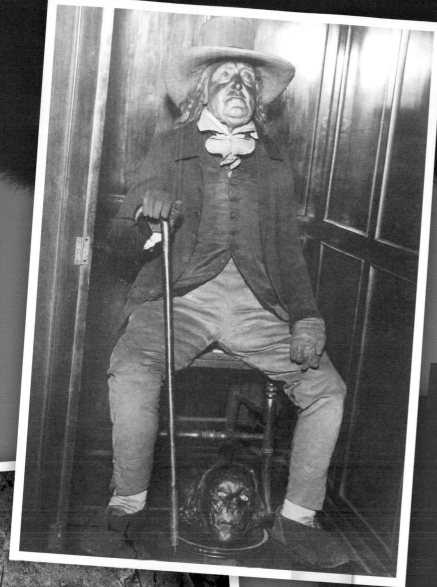

Some mummies are created naturally. In 1972, explorers in Greenland stumbled on the bodies of eight Inuit people. They had been there for over 500 years. Hundreds of years of cold, dry Arctic air had **freeze-dried** the bodies and turned them into mummies.

PEOPLE FILE

Jeremy Bentham

Born: 1748

Died: 1832

Description: Jeremy Bentham was an English writer, famous for his ideas about how society should be organized.

Famous for: When Bentham died, he left instruction that his head should be mummified and his skeleton dressed in his clothes. He can still be seen, sitting in a chair in University College, London!

GLOSSARY WORDS
freeze-dried   preserved by freezing the water a body contains, then drying it out

Ancient Egyptian
MUMMIES

Location: Ancient Egypt
Date: from 3100 BCE to about 1070 BCE, when Ancient Egypt was at the height of its power

Ancient Egypt was the center of the mummy-making world. The Ancient Egyptians had whole areas set aside for preparing mummies. The biggest of these areas was known as Necropolis, City of the Dead.

Why did the Egyptians make mummies?

Ancient Egyptian people believed that death was a gateway. They believed it led to the Afterlife, where they would live forever. They could only reach the Afterlife if their bodies were preserved after they died. This was why the Ancient Egyptians mummified their dead.

MINI FACT

Hidden among a mummy's wrappings was a plaque decorated with the Eye of Horus, an Egyptian god. It was placed over the cut in the mummy's **abdomen**. The plaque was supposed to stop evil entering the body through the cut.

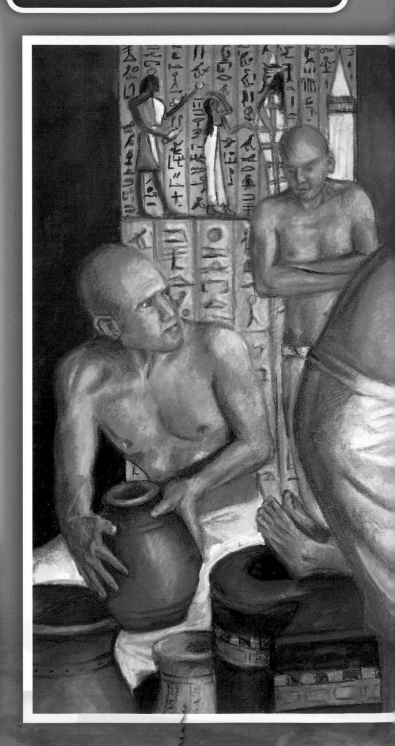

Making an Egyptian mummy

It took about 70 days to mummify a body in Ancient Egypt:

- First it was washed in *natron*, a kind of salt **solution**.

- The brain was hooked out (usually through the nose) and thrown away.

- The side of the abdomen was cut open. Organs were removed, to be mummified separately.

- The heart and kidneys were left in place.

- On about Day 15, the drying-out process began. Natron salt was packed inside the body and used to cover it. Drying took about 40 days.

- Next the body was rubbed with oils, then covered in pine **resin** to stop it from going moldy.

- Finally, the mummy was wrapped in linen cloth and sealed in resin.

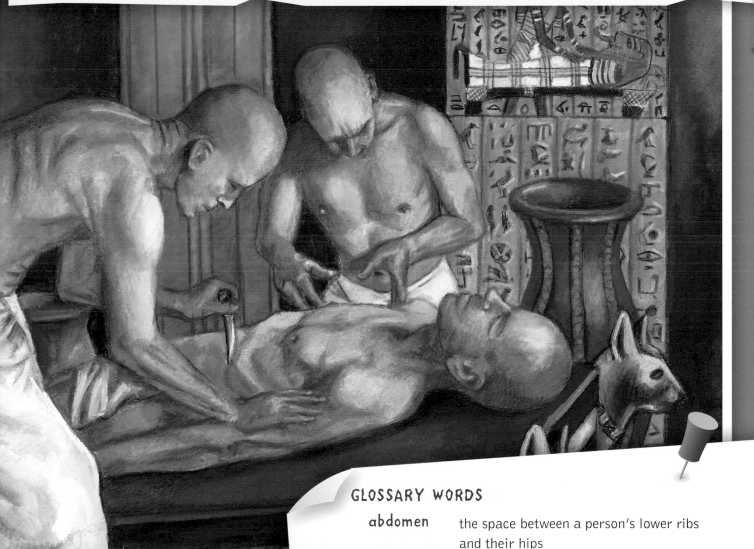

GLOSSARY WORDS

abdomen	the space between a person's lower ribs and their hips
solution	a combination of something dry with a liquid
resin	a thick, sticky liquid that flows from some trees

The tomb of Tutankhamen

The mummy of the Ancient Egyptian pharaoh Tutankhamen was first discovered in 1922. The tomb contained unimagined treasures that any tomb robber would gladly have risked his life for. But it had survived undisturbed for over 3,000 years.

An **archeologist** named Howard Carter finally discovered Tutankhamen's tomb. Carter was working for Lord Carnarvon, an English **aristocrat**. Carter had spent years searching for the undiscovered tomb of one of the pharaohs. By 1922, Lord Carnarvon had decided to stop spending money on the search. When Carter found the tomb he had been about to abandon his search and return to England.

Howard Carter

Born: Swaffham, England in 1874

Died: 1939

Description: Carter was an archeologist.

Famous for: Carter discovered Tutankhamen's tomb. He wrote several books describing his discoveries. The best known is *The Tomb of Tut-ankh-amen*.

MINI FACT

X-rays of Tutankhamen's skull show a small piece of bone stuck deep inside. Ever since this was discovered, people have wondered if it might be evidence that the pharaoh was murdered by a blow to the head.

Before Tutankhamen was sealed in his tomb, a priest would have touched his mouth, eyes, ears, and nose. This was thought to restore his senses so that he could taste, see, hear, and smell in the Afterlife. Then his coffin was sealed and he was placed in his tomb.

Discovering the tomb

Carter discovered a single step cut into a rock face. The step led to more steps, going down into a tunnel. From here, a doorway led to Tutankhamen's burial chamber. When Carter and Carnarvon broke in, they saw golden chairs, statues, jewels, and other riches everywhere. The most precious of the tomb's treasures was the **sarcophagus** containing the pharaoh's body.

The Valley of the Kings lies on the west bank of the River Nile. This side of the river was associated with death and the Afterlife. This was because the sun set (or died) in the west, before rising (being reborn) in the east.

GLOSSARY WORDS

archeologist	a person who learns about the past by studying the things its people left behind
aristocrat	a person with a high rank in society which they have inherited from their family
sarcophagus	a stone coffin

The Mummy's Curse

Since 1922, a great mystery has surrounded the discovery of Tutankhamen's tomb. Did the opening of the tomb release an ancient curse into the world?

Within days of opening the tomb, Lord Carnarvon was dead. A cut on his face became infected and poisoned his blood. People said that within minutes all the lights in Cairo went out. Back in England, Carnarvon's favorite dog howled once and dropped dead. By 1935, the Mummy's Curse was thought to have killed 21 people.

Some stories say that Tutankhamen's tomb bore a curse saying, "Death shall come on swift wings to him who enters the tomb of the pharaoh." In fact, an English writer, Marie Corelli, made up the curse in 1923.

↑ This scientist wears a mask to examine the mummy, to protect him from dangerous mold spores.

FACT FILE

Killer mummies!

Although the Mummy's Curse may not be real, mummies can still be killers!

- A mummy's wrappings may contain dangerous mold **spores**. These can survive for thousands of years.

- When the tombs are opened these spores can be disturbed.

- Once breathed in, the spores can lead to organ failure or even death.

Was the Mummy's Curse real?

Dr Mark Nelson of Monash University in Australia investigated the people "affected" by the curse. They lived to be an average of 70 years old. Ordinary people of the time lived to be 75, so if the curse did exist, it did not shorten people's lives by very much.

GLOSSARY WORDS

spores   single cells that are capable of growing

13

PEAT-BOG mummies

Location: peat bogs of Northern Europe
Date: from about 500 BCE to about 500 CE

For many years, people have been pulling mysterious bodies from Europe's peat bogs. Over 2,000 of these preserved bodies have now appeared. More may still lurk beneath the surface, waiting to be discovered.

How are the bodies preserved?

Peat is made of plants that have died and been squashed down. As the plants turn to peat, they release chemicals that kill body-rotting **bacteria**. The chemicals also preserve skin. Many peat-bog bodies have gleaming, dark-brown skin that has been stained, and preserved by the peat.

There could be bodies from thousands of years ago hidden within this peat bog, waiting to be discovered.

FACT FILE

Preserving peat bog bodies

- When peat bog bodies are exposed to the air, they start to decay.

- Most of the bodies that were first discovered fell apart very quickly.

- By the 1980s, experts knew how to keep peat bog bodies intact.

Who discovers the bodies?

For hundreds of years people have cut peat to use as fuel. It is usually peat cutters who discover the peat bog mummies. A body preserved in peat does not change over time, so it is hard to tell how long it has been buried. Sometimes the bodies appear to be quite new, which can be a shock for the peat cutters!

PEOPLE FILE

Windeby Girl

Age: 14 at time of death

Died: about 100 BCE

Description: A peat bog body discovered in Northern Germany.

Famous for: Windeby Girl's blindfolded body was found in a peat bog in Germany. A large stone and branches had been used to weigh her body down.

> Investigators do not know what happened to Windeby Girl.

GLOSSARY WORDS

bacteria   tiny creatures so small that they can only been seen through a microscope

15

Why are the peat bog bodies there?

It has taken experts years to solve the mystery of the peat bog bodies. Finding witnesses to what happened was impossible—most of the bodies are about 2,000 years old! Instead, the evidence comes from the bodies themselves. The people found in peat bogs all seemed to have suffered violent deaths. There are two likely explanations for this. The first is that the people left in the bogs were criminals who had been executed. The second is that they were religious **sacrifices**.

Tollund Man

Tollund Man is probably Europe's most famous peat bog body. He was found at Tollund **Fen** in Denmark, buried 9 feet (2.75 m) deep in the peat. He had been hanged using a leather noose.

Tollund Man, from Denmark, has the same glistening skin as many peat bog bodies. Only his head is still real—the rest of his body rotted soon after he was discovered in 1950.

16

Lindow Man

Lindow Man, a peat bog body found in England, had been hit on the head, strangled, and had his throat cut. Whoever killed him obviously wanted to do a thorough job. Other peat bog bodies have similar injuries. Some were even pinned down with wooden **stakes**.

Lindow Man is now kept in the British Museum in England.

FACT FILE

Bogs across Europe

Bogs around Europe contain all sorts of interesting remains from the past, not just peat bog bodies:

British Isles—ancient hair, fingernails, animal remains, stockings, shoes, rings, and weapons.

Denmark—Over 500 bodies were discovered in the past. Many had mysterious short haircuts—no one is sure why.

Germany—Datgen Man, whose head was found several feet from his body.

GLOSSARY WORDS

sacrifices	offerings to a god or gods
fen	a low, wet area of land, partly covered by water
stakes	sharpened sticks or posts that can be driven into the ground

FROZEN mummies

Location: the Ukok Plateau in the Altay Mountains of Siberia
Date: about 400 BCE

The ice-cold lands of the far north and the frozen tops of high mountains create their own mummies. Many of these mummies are made by accident. Living things are trapped and die in the cold. Their bodies are then preserved by freezing.

The Pazyryk were horse-riding **nomads**. They thought that when people died, they went to the **Pastures** of Heaven, a place like this high in the mountains.

The Ice Maiden

The Ice Maiden is the name of a mummy discovered in 1993. She was found on the windswept, freezing Ukok Plateau in Siberia. This land is dotted with the **funeral mounds**, or "kurgans," of an ancient people called the Pazyryk.

The Ice Maiden was discovered inside one of the burial mounds. She was covered in tattoos of animals, and wore a beautiful costume. The tattoos told a story, almost like a comic strip. The mummy was buried with six horses, which had been sacrificed at her funeral. This tells us that she was someone very important.

Who was the Ice Maiden?

Nobody knows for sure who the Ice Maiden was. Pazyryk women sometimes fought as warriors, but warriors were buried with their weapons. The Ice Maiden had no weapons with her. She was about 25 when she died, and had been in the ice for about 2,500 years. Many experts think that her unusual tattoos show she might have been a priestess, or perhaps a very famous storyteller.

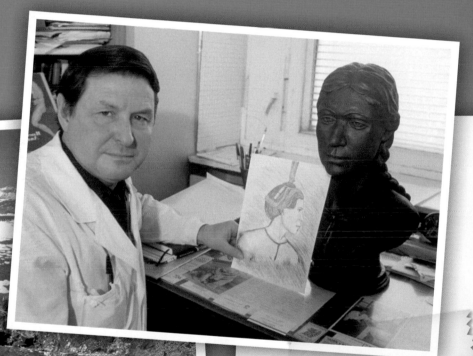

FACT FILE

Reconstructing the Ice Maiden

Scientists have been able to reconstruct the Ice Maiden's face in an effort to find out what she looked like. They have done this using the shape of her skull. They based the thickness of her skin on modern-day people's.

GLOSSARY WORDS

funeral mounds	high, round piles of earth and stones under which ancient people were buried
nomads	people who survive by raising animals and moving from place to place for new pastures
pastures	areas of land where grazing animals can feed

Ötzi the Iceman

One of the most mysterious mummies of all was discovered in 1991. High in the freezing mountains of the Otzal Alps, two climbers came upon a mummified body. They thought it might be 50 years old. In fact, Ötzi the Iceman turned out to be 5,300 years old!

Who was Ötzi?

There are many theories about who Ötzi was. Most people agree that he probably came from a village in northern Italy. He was roughly 46 when he died, which made him an old man in those days. Ötzi's skin was decorated with about 50 tattoos, which may be a sign that he was a priest.

Location: Otzal Alps, on the border between Italy and Austria
Date: about 3300 BCE

The mummy was found in the Otzal Alps. It had been frozen and preserved in the ice of a glacier for over 5,000 years. It quickly became known as Ötzi the Iceman.

What killed Ötzi?

Ötzi had a bad cut on his right hand, and he had been shot with an arrow. It seems that he was attacked and fled into the mountains to hide. There, he lay down in a **gully** and died. The snow and ice covered him until he was found in 1991.

FACT FILE

The Copper Age

Ötzi is one of the world's oldest mummies. The items found with him tell us about the time he lived in, 5,300 years ago, called the Copper Age. This was when people first began to make metal tools. Ötzi carried:

- a flat-bladed axe of copper
- a bow and some arrows
- flints and tinder for lighting fires, and a flint dagger
- a wood-framed backpack.

Ötzi got his name when an Austrian reporter combined "Otzal," the name of the mountains where he was found, with "yeti," a mysterious ape-man that is said to live in the Himalayan Mountains.

GLOSSARY WORDS

gully   a small, narrow valley

Religious mummies

The mummies of Palermo, Italy are kept in **catacombs** below one of the city's churches. There are several thousand mummies. Anyone can go and see them. The mummies are stacked on shelves, leaned against the walls, and laid in coffins, grinning out at the visitors.

Why were the mummies made?

About 400 years ago the **monks** from the church began to mummify their dead. Sicily's dry climate is perfect for making mummies. Once the internal organs had been removed, a combination of chemicals and dry air turned the bodies slowly into mummies.

The monks were very successful mummy-makers. Soon the townspeople began to pay them to mummify their dead relatives. People would then visit their dead, mummified grandparents on a Sunday afternoon!

22

Are mummies still made today?

The monks no longer mummify dead townspeople. Mummification is not common these days, and besides, they had run out of space! The monks now spend part of their time guiding tourists around the catacombs.

Today, hundreds of tourists visit the mummies in Palermo. People are very careful to leave before the catacombs close and the lights are turned out!

GLOSSARY WORDS

catacombs	underground places where dead bodies are stored
monks	members of a religious order who usually live together in a special community

Inca mummies

Location: the Inca Empire, South America
Date: 1438–1532 CE

High in the cold air of the Andes Mountains in South America, conditions are excellent for making mummies. There are plenty of mummies to be found up there. Through the years, over 100 mummies have been discovered on icy ledges or in cracks in the rock.

The mummies belonged to the Inca people. The Inca Empire ruled large areas of South America between 1438 and 1532. The Incas made **human sacrifices** as part of their religion. The mummies found in the Andes were mostly sacrificial victims of the Incas. They were killed in the high mountains to be nearer to the gods.

The cold air of the high Andes Mountains once mummified the human sacrifices of the Inca people.

PEOPLE FILE

Juanita

Age: roughly 14 at time of death

Died: about 1500

Description: Inca mummy found in Mount Ampato, Peruvian Andes

Famous for: Juanita is one of the best-preserved Inca mummies. She was discovered in 1995, wrapped in fine cloth and buried with gold and silver statues.

What were Inca mummies like?

Inca mummies were usually stored in a curled-up position. Once the bodies had been prepared, they were wrapped in leather or cloth. They might be stored in baskets or placed under huge pots. The mummies often had bright decorations. They were buried with food, clothing, and other things that might be useful in the Afterlife.

GLOSSARY WORDS

human sacrifices   deliberately killing a person as part of a religious ceremony

Who was the Sapa Inca?

The Sapa Inca was the Inca ruler. The people thought that he was a descendant of Inti, the Sun God. When the Sapa Inca died, his body was mummified. It was kept in a special palace with the other mummified Sapa Incas.

The mummies' palace was very grand. Servants waited on them there. They brought food and drink, and anything else the mummies might need. The mummies were even wrapped in blankets if it was cold.

The Sapa Inca mummies wore beautiful gold masks. No ordinary person was allowed to look at a mummy's face. Instead they had to bow down and look at the ground. Anyone who disobeyed this rule could be killed.

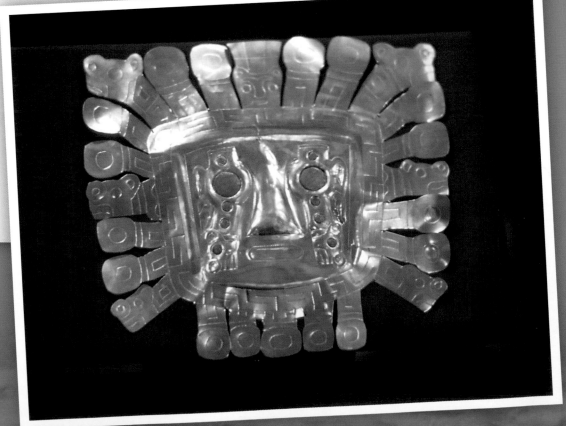

Procession of the Living Dead

Once a year the mummies left their palace, carried by their servants. The living Sapa Inca led them on the "Procession of the Living Dead" to the Temple of the Sun God. There they visited their **ancestor**, Inti, the Sun God, before being carried back to their palace.

End of the Inca mummies

Spanish soldiers conquered the Inca Empire during the 1500s. The Spanish banned mummy making. They built a church where the Temple of the Sun had stood, and stole many of the gold masks and jewels the mummies had worn.

When the Spanish conquered the Inca Empire, they stopped its people from making mummies. In four years, they managed to destroy 1,365 Inca mummies. Only those the Spanish did not discover survived to the modern day.

Desert mummies

Location: Taklamakan Desert, China
Date: from about 1000 BCE

In 1989, archaeologists in China discovered a 3,000-year-old mummy in the Taklamakan Desert. The discovery puzzled scientists and experts. The mummy had a European face and reddish hair. Why had she been in the Chinese desert centuries before the first Europeans visited China?

Soon other "European" mummies began to turn up in the desert. Many of them had been buried with their possessions. They had fine leather boots, brass jewelry, clay cups, and combs. All these things seemed to be made in a European style, rather than looking Chinese.

Cherchen Man is one of the Taklamakan mummies who shows his European background most clearly. Before the mummies were discovered it was thought that the first Europeans in China had visited in about 150 BCE.

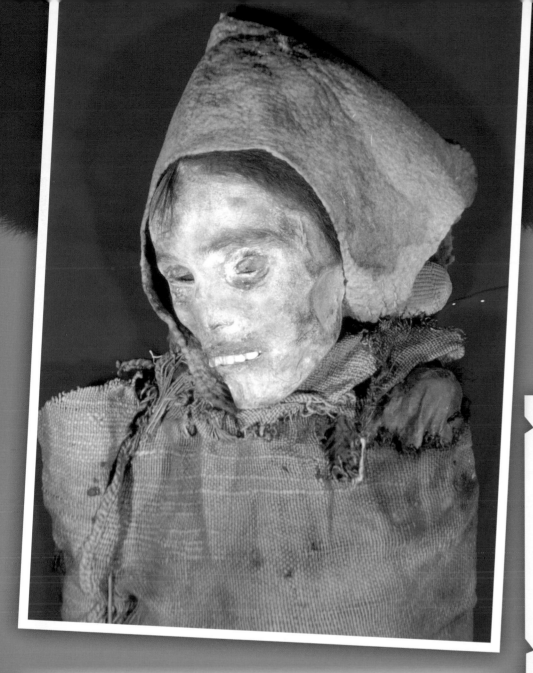

····> One mystery about the Tokarians still remains: why did they disappear without a trace?

FACT FILE

Journey to the afterlife

Some of the mummies were buried with things to help their journey to the afterlife. These included:

- a donkey's **bridle**, so they could ride in comfort

- a container for carrying water

- a loaf of bread.

Who were the desert mummies?

Writing left on the walls of their tombs provided a clue to who these mysterious people were. The writing was similar to the ancient languages of northeastern Europe. The people called themselves Tokarians. They must have moved to the east from Europe, before disappearing about 1,000 years ago.

GLOSSARY WORDS

bridle   a harness used to control an animal, especially a horse, donkey, or mule

MUMMY timeline

38,000 BCE	Dima the baby mammoth is frozen and mummified after falling into a muddy pond.
5000 BCE	Chinchorros people from Chile begin to mummify their dead.
3300 BCE	Ötzi the Iceman flees from his attackers into the Alps, where he dies and is mummified by the cold.
3100 BCE–1070 CE	Ancient Egypt is at the height of its power. All dead Egyptians are mummified.
1000 BCE	Tokarians, migrants from Europe, mummify their dead in the Chinese desert.
500 BCE–500 CE	The bodies of sacrificial victims and criminals are placed in Europe's peat bogs, where they are mummified.
400 BCE	The Ice Maiden is mummified in Siberia. People in southern Peru start to make mummy bundles of their dead.
100 BCE	Windeby Girl and Tollund Man die. "Lady Cheng," a Chinese mummy made using mercury, dies.
500 CE	Bodies placed in caves in Arizona, Tennessee and Kentucky, U.S. begin to mummify.
1000–1450 CE	Stolen pieces of mummy are used in Europe to make a paint called Caput Mortem, or "dead head," as well as medicine.
1400s–1500s CE	The Inca empire is at the height of its powers. Mummification is common.
1425 CE	The North American Iceman, Kwaday Dan Sinchi or "Long-Ago Man," is trapped in a glacier in Canada.
1500 CE	Eight Inuit people are mummified by cold and wind on Greenland.
1532 CE	The Spanish begin their conquest of the Incas. Mummy making is banned and many mummies are destroyed.
1600 to 1920 CE	Mummies are created by monks at a church in Palermo, Italy.
1832 CE	Jeremy Bentham dies and his head is mummified.
1922 CE	The tomb of Tutankhamen is opened by Howard Carter and Lord Carnarvon. Carnarvon dies soon afterward.
1924 CE	The body of dead Communist leader VI Lenin is mummified.
1939 CE	Howard Carter dies at the age of 65, apparently unaffected by the Mummy's Curse.
1952 CE	The body of Argentina's leader Eva Peron is mummified when she dies.
1959 CE	Bodies in San Bernardo, Columbia, mysteriously start to mummify.

GLOSSARY

abdomen the space between a person's lower ribs and their hips

ancestor a relative who lived a long time ago

archeologist a person who learns about the past by studying the things its people left behind

aristocrat a person with a high rank in society which they have inherited from their family

bacteria tiny creatures so small that they can only been seen through a microscope

bridle a harness used to control an animal, especially a horse, donkey, or mule

catacombs underground places where dead bodies are stored

fen a low, wet area of land, partly covered by water

freeze-dried preserved by freezing the water a body contains, then drying it out

funeral mounds high, round piles of earth and stones under which ancient people were buried

glaciers giant build-ups of compacted snow and ice in valleys

gully a small, narrow valley

human sacrifices deliberately killing a person, usually as part of a religious ceremony

monks members of a religious order who usually live together in a special community

nomads people who survive by raising animals and moving from place to place for new pastures

pastures areas of land where grazing animals can feed

peat a thick, dark-brown soil that can be burned on a fire

pharaohs rulers of ancient Egypt

preserved kept from changing

resin a sticky, thick liquid that flows from some trees

sacrifices offerings to a god or gods

sarcophagus a stone coffin

solution a combination of something dry with a liquid

spores single cells that are capable of growing

stakes sharpened sticks or posts that can be driven into the ground

INDEX